ISBN 978-1-5278-1246-8
PIBN 10894542

1 MONTH OF
FREE
READING

at
www.ForgottenBooks.com

English
Français
Deutsche
Italiano
Español
Português

www.forgottenbooks.com

Mythology Photography **Fiction**
Fishing Christianity **Art** Cooking
Essays Buddhism Freemasonry
Medicine **Biology** Music **Ancient
Egypt** Evolution Carpentry Physics
Dance Geology **Mathematics** Fitness
Shakespeare **Folklore** Yoga Marketing
Confidence Immortality Biographies
Poetry **Psychology** Witchcraft
Electronics Chemistry History **Law**
Accounting **Philosophy** Anthropology
Alchemy Drama Quantum Mechanics
Atheism Sexual Health **Ancient History**
Entrepreneurship Languages Sport
Paleontology Needlework Islam
Metaphysics Investment Archaeology
Parenting Statistics Criminology
Motivational

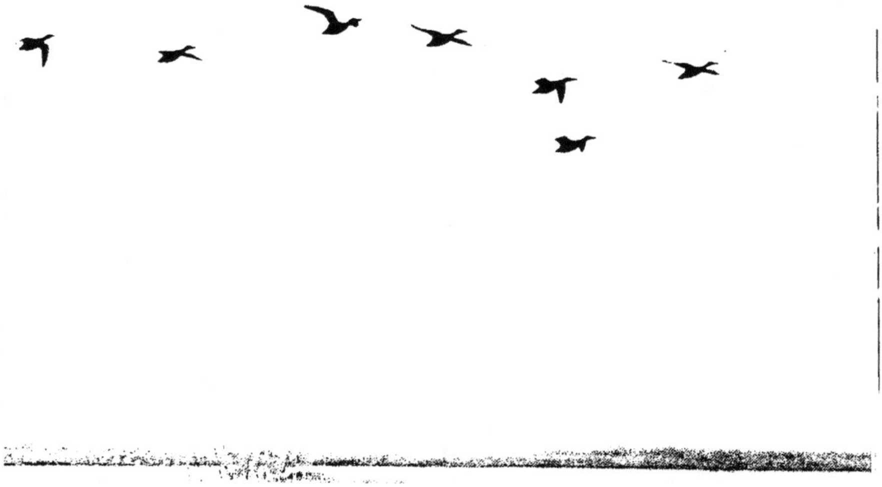

Vol. 19 Nos. 9 & 10

September-October,
1967

Conservation Pledge

I give my
pledge as an American
to save and faithfully to
defend from waste the
natural resources of
my country—its soil
and minerals, its
forests, waters
and wildlife

*Published Bi-Monthly
in the interest of conservation of Louisiana's natural resources by the
Wild Life and Fisheries
Commission, Peabody
Hall, Capitol Station.
Baton Rouge, Louisiana
70804.*

*Louisiana's teal hunters bagged an esti-
mated 96,000 teal during last year's nine
day season. Some 33,000 special teal hunting permits were issued in the state and
the bag by Louisiana hunters represented
approximately 25 per cent of the total kill
in the Mississippi and Central Flyways.
The cover shows a teal hunter watching a
flight of approaching ducks. The special
season this year from September 22
through September 30 marks the third experimental September teal season. This
represents wise management of a waterfowl resource that migrates through Louisiana before the regular duck season and
returns to the United States after all duck
hunting is over. (Cover photo by Robert
Dennie.)*

LOUISIANA WILD LIFE AND FISHERIES COMMISSION

Subscription Free to Louisiana Residents
Upon Written Request

JOHN J. McKEITHEN
Governor

DR. LESLIE L. GLASGOW
Director

L. S. ST. AMANT
Asst. Director

R. K. YANCEY
Asst. Director

LOUISIANA CONSERVATIONIST

STEVE HARMON .... Editor
McFADDEN DUFFY .... Staff Writer
EDNARD WALDO .... Staff Writer
ROBERT DENNIE .... Photographer

LOUISIANA WILD LIFE AND FISHERIES COMMISSION

JIMMIE THOMPSON, *Chairman* .... Alexandria
H. B. FAIRCHILD, *Vice Chairman* .... Sunshine
A. J. BUQUET .... Houma
JERRY G. JONES .... Cameron
JOHN E. KYLE, JR., ... Berwick
HOBSON NORRIS .... West Monroe
H. CLAY WRIGHT .... Evergreen

DIVISION CHIEFS

STEVE HARMON
Education & Publicity

JOE L. HERRING
Fish and Game

TED O'NEIL
Fur Division

ALLAN ENSMINGER
Refuge Division

ROBERT LAFLEUR
Water Pollution Control

CHARLES R. SHAW
Pittman-Robertson Coordinator

TED FORD
Oyster, Water Bottoms and Seafood

HARRY SCHAFER
Dingell-Johnson Coordinator

LARRY COOK
Chief Accountant

SAM MURRAY
Executive Assistant

LEONARD NEW
Enforcement

EDITORIAL

THE ANNUAL INCOME from commercial fisheries in Louisiana is conservatively estimated in excess of one hundred million dollars. It might be well that we consider in more detail the meaning of the economic value of the commercial seafood industry to the state. For some reason not clear to those of us working in the field of fish management, the great economic value of our fishing industry is not well known by the public, and as a result this valuable resource frequently fails to receive adequate public support for proper maintenance and management.

By comparison, the one hundred million dollar plus annual income from our fishing industry is equivalent to slightly more than one fourth of all agricultural products in the state. This means that it is equal to approximately one half of the value of all the crops sold in Louisiana, and to more than seventy five percent of the annual income from all livestock and livestock products. Thus it becomes immediately apparent that our commercial fishery products of Louisiana are equivalent to and greater than many of the important agricultural crops in the state.

Our production of shrimp alone averages from sixty to eighty million pounds annually, having a net dockside value of twenty to thirty million dollars. This great industry supports secondary industries such as ice companies, boat yards, net companies, and fuel distributors to an extent that it creates a considerably greater economic value to the state. Yet, few people realize the value of the shrimp industry to the State of Louisiana and the necessity that it be protected and managed in a manner consistent with its value. As late as 1960, because of budget limitations only one biologist could be assigned to do the technical work necessary to maintain this complex industry. In 1967, although giant strides have been made in shrimp research in Louisiana and much help has been afforded the industry by the Louisiana Wild Life and Fisheries Commission, we still have less than nine technical personnel working on shrimp. It is clear that an industry so valuable to the state, should receive the equivalent research effort and technical assistance as that which is afforded other industries of equal value.

The shrimp industry has been furnished some of the best and most practical technical information that can be obtained from limited personnel and funds.

In addition to the annual evaluation of the shrimp crop, exciting research is being conducted at the Marine Laboratory on the pond raising of

LESLIE L. GLASGOW
Director

shrimp and other sea animals. It is believed that within the near future, this method of raising shrimp can be made economically feasible and should add a new dimension to the shrimp industry of the state with equivalent economic advancement. The installation of approximately 1000 low level weirs in the marsh has semi-stabilized the water level and salinity over several thousand acres of shrimp nursery grounds. This practice alone is responsible for increasing shrimp and fish production many fold behind the dams. Many more acres of marshland should be improved in the same manner for shrimp production.

Even with such recent advances in shrimp research it behooves us to face up to the fact that such a valuable asset must be protected to the best of the state's ability. This protection should fall into two general categories.

1) The supplying of adequate funds and technical personnel to study, manage and protect the industry at all times. While considerable funds are now being spent in this direction, it is believed that we have not nearly reached a stage of funding and research activity to fully do justice to this great industry.

2) One must always look to the source and reason for the exceptional production of seafood on the Louisiana Coast. This leads us immediately to the vast marshlands and nursery grounds which border the coast of Louisiana. It has been determined biologically that this vast area is probably the greatest single reason for Louisiana's fine seafood production. It, therefore, follows that the estuarine area should be maintained in as near its natural state as possible or improved in order that production of our fishery be maintained for an indefinite period. This simply means that every activity, industry or otherwise, within the estuarine area must be examined with a critical eye toward determining how it may affect the natural production of the nursery area, both immediately and on a long term basis.

In final analysis, it is clear that the State of Louisiana and its citizens should back off and take a hard look at this valuable fishery and the area which supports it, then determine to do the utmost to protect and preserve it for the future economy and posterity of the state.   ✱

INDEX

MORE FISH FOR LOUISIANA

James T. Davis

THE ROCKFISH AND WALLEYED PIKE are returning to Louisiana. Under a new program of the fisheries section day old rockfish or striped bass fry are being flown to the state. These are released in ponds for growing and later stocking. The walleye are coming into the state as eggs which are placed into ponds soon after hatching. These two fish are doing much to cause smiles of anticipation by our avid Louisiana fishermen.

Striped bass were caught for many years by sportsmen in the "Florida parish" area. The Tchefuncte River had the best spring run. They appeared in April and May when the "sardines" (probably shad) came upriver to spawn.

In April, 1943 the Louisiana Conservationist printed a picture of a 31 pound striped bass from the Amite River. This was said to be a new record. The article further stated that the average size of "rocks" was 15 pounds. Though this is far from the 125 pounders found on the east coast, it would gladden the heart of most fishermen.

But little by little the population disappeared. Why? Were the demands of the fishermen too much to meet the supply of the spawn? This is a possibility, but, as a single female will often produce over a million eggs, it is quite doubtful. Most biologists agree that silt from gravel operations and other pollutants are the major deterrents.

Are conditions better now? We are trying to find out before restocking is started. In the meantime we have other plans for the fish. South Carolina, where we are getting the fry, has had modest success stocking lakes with striped bass. We are well on our way to a similar goal.

At Santee-Cooper Lake in South Carolina, it was noted that an overabundance of gizzard shad was controlled by the striped bass. It was feared that as the shad disappeared these monster fish would devour the game fish. Instead the striped bass declined as the shad were devoured. Furthermore, game fish such as bass, bluegill and crappie not only maintained high numbers, but grew even bigger in the company of the stripers. This apparently was due to the reduction of the harmful shad population.

We are studying lake stocking in Louisiana. As most of our old lakes have dense populations of other fish, fry or small fingerlings do not have much of a chance. Therefore, we place the fry in ponds and rear them to 3-8 inch fingerlings before stocking. The smaller ones are used for new lakes and headwaters of streams while the larger ones are used for stocking in older lakes. As only a few fish are available, stocking was started at two lakes.

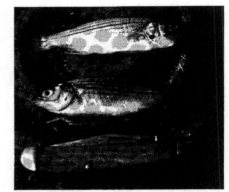

Striped bass fry being delivered to D'Arbonne Lake, 1965.

These lakes were chosen on the basis of the water quality of their tributary streams. Some streams do not have enough flow at the right time of the year for spawning. Other streams are too muddy. Still others don't have desirable sand or gravel bottoms. Other streams are periodically polluted. After careful analysis two lakes were chosen to start the program. These were D'Arbonne Lake and Toledo Bend Lake.

If the stripers in these lakes continue to survive and grow, we will soon have our own resident population. If they are able to reproduce in the tributary streams we will soon have our own hatchery right on the stream banks. This will

Striped bass fry at minimum size for successful stocking.

allow us to stock other lakes and streams in the state.

Not all lakes are suitable for striped bass. In some of these lakes the walleye will be more suitable as they do not require tributary streams for spawning. Because of this, we are studying the possibilities of stocking walleye in Louisiana lakes.

This game fish is highly sought after in most northern states. Nebraska has an excellent fishery and has been kind enough to give us fertilized eggs and fry. The eggs are flown to Monroe and placed in hatching jars. One week later the eggs begin to hatch and the hair-lake fry emerge. These fry are quite active in contrast to the fragile striped bass fry. By the second day the walleye fry are free swimming and ready for the rearing ponds.

As a game fish, the walleye can be caught any time of the year. Larger catches are made in the cooler months when most Louisiana fishing is slow. For this reason we believe it will add much to our attraction as a sportsman's paradise.

Extremely large walleye often scale over 30 pounds. Most catches are in the 10 pound or less range. As these fish grow quite rapidly a 5 pound walleye in Louisiana may be only three years old. The presence of an abundant food supply is responsible for this because walleye feed primarily on fish. In Illinois it is estimated than an adult walleye will eat over 600 shad each year. This fish may be of decided benefit for shad control in Louisiana lakes.

Rocky shoal areas are a requirement for successful spawning of the walleye. For this reason D'Arbonne Lake, Toledo Bend and Claiborne Lake where chosen for initial releases. D'Arbonne Lake has received fish for three years in an effort to establish a spawning population. Catch records to date indicate we are well on our way. A female caught during February 1967 in D'-Arbonne scaled five pounds and produced 117,000 eggs. Within three years we hope to have our own spawning population. This will eliminate the expense of flights to Nebraska to secure eggs.

Costs of these stocking programs are high at this time. If we are successful in securing our own spawning population, costs will be much less.

Pond rearing however, will remain the greatest expense. Our overtaxed hatchery facilities already produce largemouth bass, bluegill, black crappie and channel catfish. In addition, Many ponds are needed for research. By leasing a 70 acre hatchery near Delhi, we have ample room for walleye, striped bass and largemouth bass rearing this year.

Why does it take so much room? Well, each pond is stocked with 100,000 walleye or striped bass fry per acre. Two million of each, therefore, would require 40 acres of ponds. Since about 1 in 20 survive to fingerling size this 40 acres should give us 200,000 walleye and striped bass for stocking. This may sound like a pretty small return, but it's exceptionally good for fish. South Carolina reports less than 1 in 1000 survive in their lake stocking.

This, then explains, in part, why we must start so small with our stocking program. It may be several years before stripers and walleye are present in good numbers in Louisiana lakes and streams. Everything hangs in the balance on how well the first group does in these three lakes.

If the project is successful as hoped, anglers in ten years will be pulling these fighting game fish from many lakes over the state. Where lakes are unsuitable for spawning, these fish may still be able to survive and grow. If this proves true the Commission will bolster the populations with periodic stocking of fingerlings reared in the hatcheries.

Right now we are at least three years away from stocking in any additional lakes and streams. If we are successful, we will again return to the Louisiana sportsmen another "value received" for their fishing license dollar. ✤

Two year old w a l l e y e caught in D'Arbonne Lake, 1967. This fish measured over 20 inches and weighed over 5 pounds.

LOUISIANA'S LITTLE LOBSTERS

McFadden Duffy

THE PEOPLE OF LOUISIANA, from family groups to those who are engaged in the commercial production and sale of crawfish, have a virtual monopoly upon what we would like to refer to as Louisiana's Little Lobsters. With crawfish it often takes half a sack of these delicately-flavored crustacea to make a meal for a medium size family.

Oddly enough, as far as family groups are concerned there are so many produced in Louisiana each spring that anyone venturing a guess as to how many million pounds are consumed each year by family groups would find himself tottering on the verge of being fantastic, but probably falling far short of the exact figure.

At the present time intense research is being done on crawfish, particularly on methods of cultivation for commercial purposes. Progress has been made and additional progress will be made in the months and years ahead; but this article is intended to describe what crawfish mean to the average family, or individual who seeks them for his own pleasure.

Whether served boiled in the back yard or consumed on spread newspapers on a kitchen table, they are a gourmet's delight and available at no charge. One needs only a dozen nets, time on his hands, and transportation to a productive spot in order to obtain enough for himself and his family. Bait is almost dirt cheap and there are many productive baits. Some baits are more popular than others, but bait enough for a dozen nets costs less than a single pound of market crawfish.

For those with a flair for home cookery, crawfish can be fashioned in any kitchen in the state into world famous crawfish bisque, crawfish etouffe, crawfish pot pies and salads. Aside from the salads, these culinary delights take a great deal of preparation and the best suggestion is to spend a day at it and prepare enough to be frozen and saved for another day.

There are several names for Louisiana crawfish other than the scientific ones which no one is concerned with when he settles down for a feast of crawfish. Perhaps the most widely known is mudbug. We'll mention them later, just for informational purposes but this article is designed for the average family going crawfishing.

In most cases initial preparations call for the purchase of a dozen or more crawfish nets. The standard ones are sections of cord-woven mesh, the mesh-size being about a half-inch. The squares are attached at each end by inverted "V" sections of wire about the thickness of a coat hanger. There's a loop where the tops of the inverted "V" 's are joined and most persons using this type of net (marketed at about $3 a dozen) tie strips of cloth— red, white or yellow — so

This is typical crawfish country, swampy and shallow. It is ideal for placing of nets and this crawfisherman is shown heading out to place several additional nets in what he considers a likely place for the little lobster-like mud-bugs that can be fashioned into crawfish bisque, a gourmet's delight; or served boiled with hot seasoning, and prepared in many other ways.

that the nets which are submerged in about a foot of water can be easily located as the crawfisherman works his line of nets much in the manner of a fur trapper working his line of traps. A pole is used to place the nets and to retrieve them.

Some crawfishermen simply purchase a ball of cord and cut it into proper lengths, and tying the bait to the end that is cast into the water, with the other end tied to a bush. These are placed at intervals and when the crawfishermen work such lines, they gently pull in the cord and catch the feeding crawfish with a scoop net. This method is productive where crawfish are plentiful and folks using the system are skillful in retrieving the line without frightening off the crawfish.

Still other family groups have made their own "nets" which are merely two-foot-square sections of half-inch wire cloth. They are cut with tin shears and the edges are folded up about two inches. Coat hangers, swiped from the family closets are used for the supporting inverted "V" 's. They work equally as well as the woven mesh type, but they are far from common with average family groups who prefer to buy them and save themselves trouble.

While the man of the house obtains the bait

and places the bait and nets in the car, the lady of the house usually prepares a picnic luncheon and packs a portable ice chest with soft drinks and the luncheon. Crawfishing, in itself, is great sport offering an ample reward in a delicacy to be consumed later; but it is a lot more fun when turned into a picnic-outing. This is especially so when there are several children in the group who take delight in helping work the nets, but find visits to the chestful of cold drinks and sandwiches and cookies a delightful part of a crawfishing trip.

This is Louisiana's free heritage for everyone who is interested. The state's production of crawfish is tremendous and oddly enough, in Dixie, it is limited to Louisiana alone as a rewarding family pastime.

In preparation for this article, the writer fired off letters to other southern states in an effort to determine the role that crawfishing played in recreation, unsurpassed culinary enjoyment and, perhaps, as a source of an already important and growing commercial development. The first went to the Texas counterpart of the Louisiana Wild Life and Fisheries Commission. The reply, in part, read:

"I am afraid Texans don't share the enthusiasm for crawfish on the table. So far as I know, they are never sold in markets for food.

"However, large quantities are taken and sold for bait all over the state. These are almost always taken locally and as far as I know there are no crawfish centers such as in Louisiana.

"Most bait crawfish are taken from ponds by seine. Trapping is uncommon.

"The practice of crawfishing for sport is negligible. Youngsters enjoy it, taking them with a chunk of meat on the end of a line.

"Doubt if this will be of much help, but you are more than welcome to it. Good luck with your article."

The reply from Mississippi (where Louisiana crawfish are taken virtually to the state line) was also negative:

"We have checked with some of the ardent sportsmen through the state and I cannot find any section where crawfish are used in restaurants. This seems to be one custom of Louisianians that we Mississippians have not adopted."

The State of Arkansas Game and Fish Commission's reply was: "I am fully aware of the food value of the crawfish, but I am sorry to say that very few crawfish are taken in Arkansas to be used for food, and the sport of crawfishing is practically unknown here.

"Crawfish are prized for trot line bait and that is about the extent of their use."

Still working the belt of gulf state for information, the author tried Alabama. There was some encouragement that Alabamans do consume crawfish dishes, but probably from imported Louisiana crawfish.

"As far as I know," the reply read, "or can determine crawfish are not offered in restaurants in Alabama. Probably we don't have the crawfish in our waters that is used for food in

Aside from commercial operations which are steadily increasing as increased demand calls for crawfish farming, the sport is really a family one, engaged in by youngsters and older folks as well. When the season opens, countless thousands of persons head for the productive crawfish spots as often as they can.

Louisiana. We do use the small crawfish throughout Alabama as fishbait.

"I have heard from more than one source that some restaurants in the Mobile area serve Lobster dishes which are really made from crawfish, but I have been unable to get any information on this. You might write the Alabama Department of Conservation, Division of Seafoods, Bayou LaBatre, Alabama. If anyone in this Depart-

The expression on the faces of these youngsters as they sit feasting on boiled crawfish is significant enough to prove that Louisianians are introduced to the springtime delicacy when they are young and the habit is one that they never lose.

Louisiana has a unique monopoly on edible craw-fish in the deep South. Crawfishing as a sport is found nowhere else in the belt of northern gulf states, or Arkansas. There's no license necessary and no limit as to how many of the tasty crustacea can be taken during the spring season. All that is necessary are nets such as shown above, bait, and a tub or sack to hold the catch.

Nets are baited and most crawfishermen tie strips of bright cloth on the top of the wire frame in order to locate the submerged nets which are placed in ditches and swampy areas at intervals much in the manner of furtraps. The crawfisherman works his nets much in the fashion of the fur trapper, but more frequently; collecting his catch in a sack or tub as he moves along.

ment would, that Division probably could give you detailed information."

Next, we wrote to the Florida Game and Fresh Water Fish Commission. Their reply was as follows:

"Your recent letter concerning crawfish has been referred to us for attention. (Florida State Board of Conservation).

"Before sending you a lot of literature and information on our crawfish, perhaps we had better determine which one you are concerned with.

"Could you give us the Latin name of your animal? Since the Florida crawfish (a salt water form) has, as far as I know, not been found in Louisiana coastal waters, and since you have a 'crawfish' that is indigenous to your fresh waters, I am afraid that information on our animal would be of little help to you. Little help, that is, unless your famous bisque is made of our crawfish.

"We'll gladly help you if you let us know the exact crawfish which currently tickles the Louisiana palates."

There was no need to reply. A canvass of all the coastal states from Texas to Florida and a query from Arkansas for good measure revealed that the Pelican state has an odd monopoly on edible crawfish and that the millions of pounds taken annually represent not only a valuable commercial resource but also one of the most inviting family outings.

Any crawfishing trip afield is fun for youngsters from five years upwards to bonneted grandmothers who merely sit by the bank of a roadside ditch and watch. ✺

Attention Fish Farmers!

Anyone engaged in the propagation of fish, shiners, crawfish, turtles or frogs to sell is required by law to obtain annually a Resident Fish Farmer's License. This license costs ten dollars ($10.00) and is good for a calendar year (January 1-December 31).

Application for the fish farmer's license with a check or money order for the above amount should be mailed to Fish and Game Division, Louisiana Wild Life and Fisheries Commission, Capitol Station, Baton Rouge, Louisiana 70804.

WILDLIFE-O-GRAM

WILDLIFE AGENT HONORED

Gilmand J. Landry, a wildlife enforcement agent of the Louisiana Wild Life and Fisheries Commission was honored by the American Legion Post 338 at a banquet at Delcambre, Louisiana, August 12, according to Leonard New, chief of the Enforcement Division.

The banquet was given in recognition of the work done by Landry and other Peace Officers and stressed the work done by Landry, Sheriff Euda Delcambre of Vermilion Parish, and Rivers Bourque, Chief of Police of Delcambre.

Landry has been cited on many occasions for his work in conservation education among the youth of the section and extra curricula work done with sportsmen's clubs and youth organizations.

OUTDOOR WRITERS ASSOCIATION OF AMERICA ELECTS

Homer Circle, Rogers, Ark., was elected president of the Outdoor Writers Association of America during the organization's 1967 annual convention held this summer at Price Albert National Park, Waskesiu, Saskatchewan. Homer is Special Features Editor of Sports Afield magazine and has served as a vice president of the OWAA during the past year. He succeeds John Gartner, Editor of "Western Outdoors" magazine, in the presidency of the 1,200 member organization.

Other members elected as officers or board members of OWAA for the coming year were: vice-presidents—Hurley Campbell, Baton Rouge, La.; Bob Munger, Columbus, Nebraska; and Howard Gray, Seattle, Wash.; and Secretary—Seth L. Myers, Sharon, Pa.

EDITOR'S BOOK REVIEW

FAMILY CAMPERS' COOKBOOK—by Bill Riviere. As more and more Americans join the camping fraternity, a book for the camping family had to come and Author Bill Riviere and his family have produced an informative and interesting document in this 244 page endeavor. Louisiana outdoorsmen will rejoice when they reach the chapter of the DUTCH OVEN. I agree with the author that the true Dutch Oven is the one made from cast iron. Any other type is a mere imitation. It is in this pot that comes the delectable gumbos, stews, bisques, jambalayas, soups-ad infinitum—all favorites of the Louisiana camping family. Published by Holt, Rinehart and Winston, New York.

FAST WORK ON SPRING BAYOU

The Commission obtained the Spring Bayou Wildlife Management Area in Avoyelles Parish in November, 1966. It has already announced there will be duck hunting in the area, squirrel and rabbit hunting without dogs, and a total of five days of deer hunting for bucks only, the latter on a daily permit basis as on other wildlife management areas. Considerable boundary surveying has been done and a 1200-acre "rest area" to hold ducks on the management area has established. This clearly indicates fast work on the part of the Commission in providing public hunting less than a year after purchase of the area.

Modern-day floating buggies as pictured above have solved many of the problems encountered in marsh traveled by the earlier slat-wheel buggies.

One of the most popular modern day type of marsh mud boats utilizes a small air-cooled engine and weedless propeller.

They Ply The Marsh

Allan Esminger

T HE FOUR and one-half million acres of marshland located in the southern portion of Louisiana can be described as a flat grass-covered area interlaced with numerous bayous, lakes, canals, ponds and potholes. The majority of these coastal marshes are not stable enough to support tree growth; although on some areas located near bayou banks, lake edges and shorelines, a narrow band of oaks, cypress and hackberry is found. These ridges were selected as home sites by the settlers of this area in the 18th century. Some farming and cattle were raised here although the majority of their revenue came from trapping and fishing.

Marsh travel at that time was very primitive. Sailing vessels were used on the large lakes and navigable rivers, and the pirogue, which was copied from the Indian's canoe, provided the only method of transportation into the more remote areas of the marsh. Although the pirogue has been modified many times since it was first used by the Indians, it is still one of our main methods of transportation in remote areas of marshland. This provided a means of travel through the water ways, but walking and in some more firmer marshes horses were used to a limited extent to tranverse these extensive grassland meadows.

It was not until the invention of the marsh

Air boats have been used successfully in some of the delta marshes by the Wild Life & Fisheries Commission to capture white-tailed deer for restocking purposes.

Another modern-day buggy is the track type which has aluminum slats attached to drive chains which travel over flotation tanks. This type of buggy is well suited to varied aquatic type of marshes

buggy in the early 1930's that man could cross many miles of these marshes in one day's time. This was a very primitive slat wheel machine mounted on a tractor frame. In its infancy, it was used by trappers to cut trails through the dense marsh vegetation and also by alligator hunters during the summer months. Although this buggy had many advantages it also had several disadvantages; first of all it could not float. This again restricted the early marsh traveler. Once bogged it was powerless and many a man hour was spent digging the large slat wheels from the bottom of a pond or bayou. Standard equipment carried on the old slat wheel buggies was a good supply of timbers to provide crossing for ditches and bayous, also several gallons of motor oil was carried just in case these ditches were deep and water was taken into the base of the engine during the crossing. If this occurred the oil was then drained and new oil was added to the engine, then the trip was continued. Crossings such as this, took several hours to accomplish.

It was not until the late 1930's that the first floating buggy was built. Flotation was accomplished by using large rubber tires, with rear axle steering. It was later improved upon and the rear axle steering was abandoned. This led to the development of the hollow drum type steel wheel buggy with front axle steering.

By this time the oil companies had expanded their seismic operations in the coastal marshes, and a floating type marsh buggy was very much in demand. Mudboat ditches were plowed by slat wheel buggies. This made easier, faster and cheaper travel by boat, but the ditches limited the range of the buggy because they could not cross them. Numerous access canals were being cut to new well sites and finally joining into a vast network of waterways. As these networks of canals

spread, the usefulness of the slat wheel buggy became obsolete.

It was not until after World War II, were such improvements added as four wheel drive, and power steering. Also, the chain drive track buggy was at this time in its infancy and later proved to be the most versatile of the three.

Along with the advancement of the marsh buggy, outboard motors were fast becoming the byword in deep water travel. Also, trappers were using mud boats to navigate the shallow marsh ditches. These flat-bottomed, water propeller driven boats were capable of operating in shallow water as each had a self contained water reservoir and cooling system.

Today, people who are involved in marsh travel have at their disposal numerous types of conveyances each suitable for a specific job. Outboard motors, mud boats, airboats and marsh buggies to name a few and helicopters are being used to a limited extent by the oil companies to carry supplies and crews to well sites in remote marsh location.

The evolution of marsh travel from the early period to the present time has spanded a period of not more than thirty-five years. This all came about in a relatively short period of time due to the relentless pursuit of man's needs, for trapping, fishing, and later for his pleasure of hunting and fishing, but mainly for the riches in oil and mineral deposits these marshes held. · ✱

Helicopters equipped with flotation gear are the ultimate in modern-day marsh conveyance.

Pass-A-Loutre Waterfowl Management Area

The Louisiana Wild Life and Fisheries Commission will again operate the public hunting program on the Pass-a-Loutre Waterfowl Management area during the 1967-68 season.

All of the public camps have been renovated since Hurricane Betsy, and the marshes are in good condition to attract large numbers of wintering waterfowl to the area again this winter.

Detailed information regarding the procedure for applying and hunting dates will be published in the November-December issue of the LOUISIANA CONSERVATIONIST.

Wildlife Shorts

Five kinds of sea turtles contribute to Louisiana's supply of market turtle meat. The gray sea turtle, smallest of the five Atlantic and Gulf sea turtles, seems to be the most common kind along our coast. They prefer to lay their eggs on the loose sandy beaches of the Chandeleur Chain, rather than on the more compact beaches west of the active delta of the Mississippi river.

The world's fastest dog is not the greyhound but the saluki which has been clocked at speeds up to 43 miles per hour.

Boundary Survey of Red River and Spring Bayou Areas

J. B. Kidd and David F. Taylor

THE LOUISIANA WILD LIFE AND FISHERIES Commission due to an accelerated program to secure more hunting and fishing areas for the general public's use, recently purchased two wildlife management areas where development practices will soon be initiated to improve wildlife populations. These two areas are known as the Spring Bayou Wild Life Management Area, 11,200 acres, and the Red River Wild Life Management area, 12,600 acres in size. The Spring Bayou unit is located in Avoyelles Parish on the outskirts of Marksville and the Red River area lies on the southern extremity of Concordia Parish with the Red River as it's southern boundary.

The first order of business after securing a wildlife management area is correct and permanent boundary identification. This important job is now in progress by professional surveyors hired by the Louisiana Wild Life and Fisheries Commission for this specific purpose. This work is proceeding as well as can be expected, due to the particularly difficult topography to work in, high back water conditions this spring and the extreme difficulty in locating lines and proving

corners which were last established in the 1850's, it is impossible to anticipate a closing date for this work. It is hoped, however, that both areas will have permanent completed boundaries by early October when the major portion of the hunting seasons resume.

Red River Area

The surveying of the Red River Wildlife Management Area began April 3, 1967. The contract to do this work was awarded to A. J. Brouillette of Natchitoches.

The boundaries of Red River Wildlife Management Area consist of approximately 17 miles of land boundary and 14 miles along Cocodrie Bayou and Red River. As of this date the surveying is approximately eighty percent complete. All work was halted on May 15, 1967 due to high water. As soon as high waters recede and weather conditions permit, work will resume on the area.

Following completion of the surveying, Commission personnel will mark the boundary with white paint and erect 12" x 13" metal boundary signs on trees at approximately 150 foot intervals. At the present time, signs have been erected along

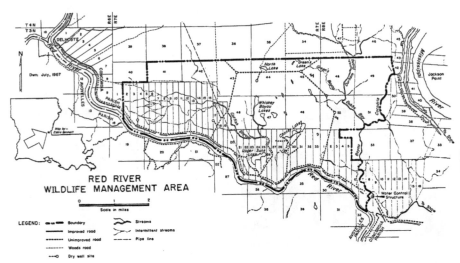

RED RIVER
WILDLIFE MANAGEMENT AREA

Scale in miles

LEGEND:
- Boundary
- Improved road
- Unimproved road
- Woods road
- Dry well site
- Streams
- Intermittent streams
- Pipe line

e Boa

Spring Bayou
Wild Life. Mgt. Area

Completed boundary ++++++++
Incompleted boundary ————

approximately two miles of land boundary and along approximately four miles of Cocodrie Bayou. A 48" x 36" entrance sign has been erected on the west end of the levee which traverses nine miles along the area's southern boundary. Once surveying is completed, another entrance marker will be placed on the east end of the levee. Also, approximately six miles of boundary lines have been identified with white tree marking paint.

Spring Bayou Area

Boundary identification of the Spring Bayou Wild Life Management Area began May 22, 1967. This work is being conducted by Mr. Blanchard Marchand of Cottonport, who is the appointed official surveyor of Avoyelles Parish. At this writing 1/8 of the boundary has been defined, painted and marked with metal signs. As the survey crew establishes permanent lines, the area supervisor, Billy K. James, follows marking the perimeter with bright orange paint. At 150

foot intervals, metal signs are also erected along the established lines. Two 3' x 4' entrance markers have been erected on the two major access routes into the area. These two signs are placed at vantage points on Boggy Bayou on the north and Old River on the South and are clearly visible as you enter the management area by these routes.

It is estimated that the Spring Bayou boundaries run for a distance of some 30 miles. Several miles of the boundary extend through permanent water with dense stands of button willow and submerged aquatics. There are four areas where the boundary crosses a major lake or stream. This is particularly difficult terrain for the survey crew to walk in and progress is slow. All obstacles however, will be overcome, and when the job is completed the boundaries will be clearly defined and marked so that there will be no dispute where the property of the wildlife management area exists.   ✦

SHRIMP CANNERS CELEBRATE

The 100th anniversary of the canning of shrimp commercially was celebrated July 12th at the Marine Laboratory located on Grand Terre Island. The first successful canning of shrimp commercially was done by George W. Dunbar and Sons near this island. To commemorate this occasion the American Shrimp Canners Association, comprised chiefly of Louisiana firms and other firms around the Gulf, staged a centennial celebration at the Marine Laboratory. President Emile Lapeyre, Jr., of Houma, Louisiana, presented an appropriate plaque to the State of Louisiana, Wild Life and Fisheries Commission, for displaying in the laboratory building. Present for this ceremony were approximately 125 people including State Representatives, officials of the Bureau of Commercial Fisheries, U. S. Fish and Wildlife Service, Parish and Municipal officials, representatives of the news media and interested citizens. The association made arrangements for and had on display early types of equipment used in the shrimp canning industry which attracted much interest. The climax of the centennial celebration was an old-fashioned Louisiana shrimp boil.

Jimmie Thompson, Chairman of the Louisiana Wild Life and Fisheries Commission, is shown receiving plaque from Emile Lapeyre, Jr. president of the American Shrimp Canners Association.

One of the fisheries research ponds at the marine laboratory was drawn down and the shrimp crop was harvested prior to the ceremonies so that interested visitors could see some of the work in progress at the marine laboratory.

100 YEARS OF PROGRESS

Early arrivals at the Marine Laboratory a r e seen getting off one of the boats.

Dr. Leslie L. Glasgow discussed the importance of shrimp and other renewable marine resources to the economy of Louisiana.

After the pond is drawn down the shrimp are seined and put in plastic cans for measurement and weight evaluations. Considerable effort must be expended to obtain all the shrimp from the pond which was stocked with 5,000 brown shrimp initially.

SOME FACTS AND FIGURES ABOUT
THE 1966-67 DEER SEASON

DAN DENNETT, JR.

FOR THE PAST DECADE, hunters have witnessed continued improvement in deer hunting conditions here in Louisiana. This has been brought about primarily as a result of the highly successful deer restocking program conducted by the Louisiana Wild Life and Fisheries Commission. Regular deer seasons and flourishing deer herds are now commonplace in most parts of the state. At this time there are very few acres of suitable deer habitat that do not support a deer herd. As the white-tailed deer gradually became re-established throughout the state and populations reached huntable proportions, a new era of deer hunting came about. In recent years the popularity of this important sport has increased by leaps and bounds and the annual deer harvest has grown accordingly.

In an effort to understand more about our vast army of deer hunters, the annual deer harvest, and the relationships between the two, the technical staff of the Commission has designed and initiated a survey of deer harvest information concerning the 1966-67 deer hunting season. The results of this survey are highly enlightening and should be of interest to the sportsman of our state in general, and to the deer hunter in particular.

Before entering a discussion of the results of our survey it would be best to briefly acquaint the reader with the procedure used in gathering the information that was needed.

Mail questionnaires were sent to randomly selected deer hunters throughout the state. These selections were made from the records of licenses sold in each parish. The number of hunters from each parish receiving questionnaires was determined statistically prior to the random selections. By distributing the questionnaires in this manner, we were able to obtain information from all categories of hunters from each parish in the state.

On the basis of information gathered during this survey, we determined that there were 111,611 deer hunters during the 1966-67 deer hunting season. Of this number, 110,950 hunted with the gun while 7,706 professed to be bow hunters. This high number of bow hunters is not surprising when you consider the growing popu-

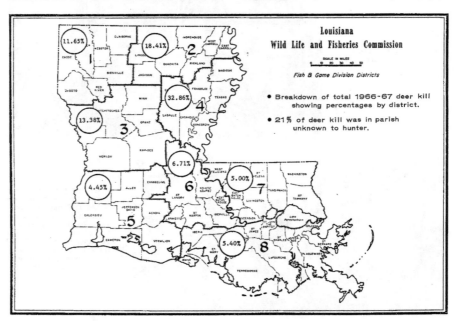

Louisiana
Wild Life and Fisheries Commission

SCALE IN MILES
0   10   20   30   40   50

Fish & Game Division Districts

● Breakdown of total 1966-67 deer kill showing percentages by district.

● 21% of deer kill was in parish unknown to hunter.

larity that this new sport has enjoyed here in the deep South during recent years. We might also add that the high number of gun hunters is well within reasonable limits expected because of the increased interest in deer hunting. Our estimates show that the total number of deer hunters of either type, the bow or the gun, increased by 13,853 hunters, or 14.2%, since the 1965-66 deer season. If the popularity of deer hunting continues at its present rate of growth, game managers of the future will have to employ the best available techniques in order to meet the demand.

One of the primary objectives of this survey was to determine the total annual harvest for the 1966-67 season. When the last button of computer was punched and the results were calculated, it was found that 32,501 deer were taken by the legal deer hunter during this season. This represents the best deer hunting season ever held in the State of Louisiana. Further data showed that 29,573 bucks were taken, as well as 2,928 does. While the number of does does not seem to be very high, it must be remembered that this sex of deer could be legally taken only on certain game management areas and in specific portions of Madison and Tensas Parishes.

It was also highly desirable to determine how the annual deer harvest was distributed throughout the state. For the sake of simplicity, the harvest has been broken down by district. District IV, which includes most of the high deer populations found in the Mississippi River delta, accounted for approximately 32.86% of the total deer killed. Going a little deeper into the success of the area along the Mississippi River in Northeast Louisiana, we find that East Carroll, Madison, Tensas, and Concordia Parishes accounted for 30.87% of the total deer killed during the 1966-67 season. This is not surprising because of the fact that this area has long been noted as being heavily populated with deer and having a high hunter utilization of this resource. Our survey does show that other districts in the state are also coming into their own as deer producing areas. District II contributed 18.41% of the total deer killed; District III provided 13.38%, and District I showed a total of 11.65%. Those districts in the southern part of the state made notable contributions to the total statewide harvest. District V showed 4.45%, District VI had 6.71%, District VII accounted for 5.00%, and District VIII provided 5.40%.

From these figures we can easily see that deer hunters are experiencing good success in widely scattered areas throughout the state. There was a time in the not too distant past when the parishes along the Mississippi River in Northeast Louisiana, previously mentioned, provided a large percent of the total annual deer killed. As the deer herds in the other sections of the state develop, increasing amounts of hunting pressure will doubtlessly be placed upon them. It is fortunate indeed that these other parts of the state are developing into areas of good hunting success because of the need created by large scale land clearing operations in the hardwood regions.

One of the more interesting aspects of the data gathered by our survey is that of hunter success. It was found that only 20.6% of the hunters are successful. Of those hunters that are successful, 14% took one deer, 4.3% bagged two deer, and only 2.3 were able to fill their legal limit of three deer per season. Judging from these figures, "Mr. Average Deer Hunter" should consider himself in a very select group if he managed to pack any venison in the deep freeze. It was found that the average hunter spent 8.4 days pursuing the white-tailed deer. This is based on the data showing a total of 943,012 days spent deer hunting in Louisiana during the season measured. One of the most astounding calculations we can make concerning the time expended by hunters in relation to the total kill is that there was an average of 29.1 efforts expended for every deer killed.

Applications of certain data gathered allowed us to calculate the total number of deer killed in any given parish of the state. We were also able to compute the total number of deer killed by those persons purchasing a big game license in that parish. Here we can make the assumption that most persons will purchase their big game license in the parish where they normally reside, which is no doubt true in practically all cases. We find that parishes containing large metropolitan areas showed understandably very low or no deer kill. We also find that many persons who purchased big game licenses within these parishes of a metropolitan area reported successful deer hunts. We must then conclude that the people from this type of area must at least leave their home parish in order to find areas that provide successful hunting. This situation further emphasizes the need for more intensive management of our deer herds in every possible portion of this state.

There are many, many more statistics concerning the 1966-67 deer harvest which we could expound upon, but those which we have just given are the backbone of our most recent deer kill survey. These data provide the administrator, the law maker, and the biologist a much better understanding of Louisiana deer hunting. It is only through this increased knowledge and better understanding of all of the factors affecting game populations that we will be able to meet our obligations to the hunters of this state. ✦

Wildlife Shorts

The Louisiana white-tail deer, the state's largest game animal, along with the mule deer of other climes, are the two most abundant game animals found on the North American continent.

The reason why antlers shed by deer each year are not abundant is that they are eaten by porcupines, mice and other rodents, mainly because they are high in calcium content.

SHELL PLANTING FOR OYSTER CULTCH CONTINUED IN 1967

Max Summers

O N MAY 27TH TWO FLUSH DECK BARGES heaped high with clam shells were maneuvered into position a few hundred feet from Half-Moon Island in the westernmost portion of Mississippi Sound. These initial activities marked the beginning of the 1967 shell planting operation. This scene was repeated many times through June 6th until a total of 15,150 cubic yards of clam shells had been planted on 500 acres of water bottoms at this St. Bernard Parish site.

June 7th found a continuation of this program; however, the setting had shifted to Black Bay located in Plaquemines Parish between Bayou Terre Boeuf and the mouth of Aux Chene (Oak) River. Here, at this location, 26 barge loads of clam shells totaling some 18,182 cubic yards were planted on a 550 acre site.

These two planting areas were carefully selected by representatives of the Louisiana Oyster Dealers and Growers Association and representatives of the Oysters, Water Bottoms and Seafoods Division of the Louisiana Wild Life and Fisheries Commission. The final sites chosen were in the natural seed oyster producing areas east of the Mississippi River. Each area selected had good bottom characteristics, suitable water conditions and a historical record of seed oyster production.

The clam shells planted were dredged in Lake Maurepas because it was desirable to use clam shells at least ¾ inch or larger in size. This area is noted for its deposits of large clam shells. These larger shells increase the probability of a high spat catch. Of the total 33,333 cubic yards of clam shells planted in both areas, over 90 per cent of the shells were ¾ inch or larger.

The total planting effort was made possible by a Federal Aid Program provided for by Public Law 88-309, the Commercial Fisheries Research and Development Act which makes available matching funds for commercial fisheries programs by various groups or agencies qualifying for these appropriations. Funds from the P. L. 88-309 Program were utilized on a 50-50 cost-sharing basis in this shell planting effort.

Maintaining seed oyster stock is an effective means to assure continued oyster production in future years. This year's planting along with previous year's activities will aid the oyster industry in returning to a more optimum level of production after the ravages of Hurricane Betsy in 1965.

Louisiana oysters belong to the group of bivalves (two-shell) animals which discharge their eggs directly into the water. Fertilization occurs

Barge loads of clam shells are brought to the planting site by tug boats. Here the loads are being measured to determine the volume of shells the barges are carrying.

Shells are sprayed overboard by water pumped at pressure exceeding 90 lbs. per square inch. This water velocity is necessary to get good distribution of the cultch material. Several hundred yards of shells can be planted in one hour using three spray heads.

The clam shells are measured to determine size. At least 90 per cent of all the shells planted must be 3/4 inch in size. These large shells will provide excellent cultch and increase the probability of a good spat catch.

outside the body of the organisms. This spawning activity occurs when water temperatures are between 20° C. and 34° C. (approximately 70° to 85° Fahrenheit). In Louisiana there are two peaks of oyster reproduction; the first comes in May and June, the second peak is in September and October.

Studies indicate a healthy female oyster can produce several million eggs during the spawning season. A few hours after the eggs are fertilized, the microscopic egg has divided into an aggregate of cells. Vibrating hair called "cilia" appear on the developing baby oysters. This stage is free-swimming and moves with the prevailing currents and tides. Within a three-day period, the embryos develop two tiny shells. These grow larger and heavier as the larval oysters continue development. At this time, the small oysters must find a hard clean surface on which to attach, otherwise, they will settle into the mud and perish. Clam shells make ideal cultch or provide excellent surfaces on which the baby oysters

Good shell distribution and adequate coverage of the entire planting site is of particular importance if a good spat catch is to result.

(spat) can catch, or cement themselves.

Oyster spat caught on the cultch material planted in May and June, 1967, will provide seed oysters for the fishermen in September of 1968. The May-June and September-October spat fall should assure Louisiana oyster fishermen ample opportunity to harvest good quantities of seed oysters when the two areas are opened to fishing.

Both planting sites will be sampled after each spatfall season to check the catch success and to evaluate the effectiveness of the overall project.

The results of these examinations will be presented later in a more detailed and comprehensive report.   ✛

Wildlife Shorts

The woodcock, a seasonal visitor to Louisiana, seldom sees what it eats. By driving a three-inch bill into the mud, its sensitive tip feels out earthworms, the principal food of the woodcock.

Turtles have no teeth, but their jawbones are often very sharp and hard.

There are approximately 10,000 to 12,000 living species of birds. Human curiosity about them is greater than ever. It is estimated that in North America, 250,000 persons own at least one book about birds. In Great Britain, the figure is 1,000,000 persons.

The number of accidental deaths due to sporting arms has dropped a third in spite of the growth in population and the doubling of licensed hunters during the past 30 years.

An insurance company reports that in a five-year study of claims, hunting was 16th on the list of "dangerous" sports. In that period, there were 777 hunting claims and 4,318 from football. Hunting was also outnumbered by 824 accidents in theatres, concerts and churches.

There are roughly 20,000 federal, state, county and local firearms laws and ordinances on the books at present.

The Baltimore Oriole, a visitor to Louisiana, is said to have been given its name by the naturalist Linnaeus in honor of Lord Baltimore, whose family colors, orange and black, the male bird wears.

There are well over five hundred species of parrots, but only one, the Carolina Parakeet, is known to have lived and bred in the United States. Once seen all over Louisiana, this gorgeous orange, yellow and green bird, was once abundant along the Atlantic coastal plain from Virginia to Southern Florida, and also from the midwest to the Gulf Coast. It is now believed to be extinct.

The Screech Owl doesn't screech at all but instead gives a low-pitched tremulous wail, half whistle and half voice, that floats eerily on the Louisiana night air.

Bag Limits and Seasons on Squirrels

J. B. Kidd, Biologist

LOUISIANA HAS TRADITIONALLY had a long squirrel season with a relatively large bag limit. During the past 20 years Louisiana's squirrel season has run roughly for a 3 month period with bag limits varying from a low of 6 to a high of 10 daily. For the past 6 consecutive years, 1960-1966 the bag has been 8 daily with the season opening on the first Saturday in October and extending through January 10. This current trend seems to satisfy most hunters and as shall be pointed out is biologically sound as well.

While a large bag limit of squirrels is available to hunters annually, the average take per hunting trip throughout the state is considerably lower. During the 1953-54 hunting season 1352 bag checks were made in 19 parishes of the state. These hunters killed 2497 squirrels for an average kill per hunting trip of 1.9 squirrels. During the 1954-55 season 1877 hunters averaged killing 2.7 squirrels per trip; in the 1955-56 season 1418 hunters checked had killed an average of 1.7 squirrels per hunt; the 1956-57 season revealed that 2164 hunters averaged killing 1.6 squirrels per hunting effort; and during the 1957-58 season 844 hunters bagged an average of 1.7 squirrels per trip. In addition to these state-wide averages, game management area hunts from 1954 through 1965 show that hunters averaged killing about 2 squirrels per hunting effort. This figure was determined from making more than 50,000 individual hunter bag checks on controlled managed hunts where every person's bag is checked at the completion of each hunt.

The above data clearly demonstrated that the size of the bag limit has little to do with the hunters average kill. Hunters may boast of their ability to kill squirrels, but in actuality they are relatively few who are able to kill a limit of 8 squirrels. Very accurate records were kept on 16,811 bag checks in the Thistlethwaite G.M.A. from 1958-1965. This data shows that only 4.2 percent of the hunting efforts resulted in limit kills. Further information shows that 27 percent didn't net a single squirrel; (see table below) and it is further demonstrated that 75% of the hunts resulted in netting 3 squirrels or less!

Considerable controversy exists among hunters concerning opening dates of the squirrel season. Collected information shows that the squirrel population reaches its peak during early October and squirrels are easier killed at this time of year than any other. It is realized that some infant animals may still be nursing at this time, but a delay until late October will only serve to reduce the hunters' chance of successful hunting. There is actually no month of the year when some

Hunter Success Classes
16,811 Bag Checks
Thistlethwaite G.M.A.—1958-1965

Percent Hunters Killing 0 Squirrels	27.2
,, ,, ,, 1 ,,	20.1
,, ,, ,, 2 ,,	16.0
,, ,, ,, 3 ,,	11.6
,, ,, ,, 4 ,,	8.2
,, ,, ,, 5 ,,	5.4
,, ,, ,, 6 ,,	4.8
,, ,, ,, 7 ,,	2.5
,, ,, ,, 8 ,,	4.2

breeding cannot be detected. This is especially noticeable during mild winters when breeding may be quite prevalent during the winter months. The early October season allows hunters to still hunt while the squirrels are feeding in the trees and it is during this time that the bulk of the season's squirrel kill is made (75%-80%). When all factors are weighed carefully it is both logical and biologically sound to open Louisiana's squirrel season in early October.

The length of the squirrel season is allowed to extend through the tenth of January. This season is purposely set in this manner to benefit the hunter who likes to use dogs while hunting squirrels. During December and January ground feeding squirrels may be easily found with a dog. There is some opposition to the use of dogs by "died-in-the-wool" still hunters. Those opposing the use of dogs may think that squirrel hunting at this time of the year is a serious detriment to future populations. It is granted that females are beginning to breed at this time and pregnant animals may be found in the population. But the kill by the dog hunter is negligible where the overall population is considered. A total of 3229 bag checks made in the field in 1954 and 1955 show that only 3.5% of the hunters owned squirrel dogs. There never has been conclusive proof that dog hunting caused any serious detrimental effects on future squirrel populations. Since it is the responsibility of the Commission to provide as much hunting recreation as possible to hunters, dog hunting will continue as long as undesirable effects cannot be measured.

The pattern of regulations set by the Louisiana Wild Life and Fisheries Commission at present is to open the season the first Saturday in October and allow it to extend to January 10. This beginning gives most hunters an equal opportunity to bag a few bushytails before they become too wild and satisfies the needs of the still hunters. The late extension into January will also permit the dog hunter to exercise his perrogative in hunting with dogs. ✱

Lloyd Moreau, left, well known local fisherman, had to take a back seat to his lovely daughter; Jeannie Moreau Barillas. Lloyd's daughter came to visit from her home in San Salvadore and went home with the first place Sailfish as well as the award as the Outstanding Fisherette.

Otto Candies, right, president of the 1967 rodeo introduces the president elect for the 1968 classis T. J. Fuson as Urban Wilkenson, right rear, general chairman looks on.

White Marlin—W. Wilson, *South Pass, 62-8
Redfish—Louis Wolfort, New Orleans, 30-8
Red Snapper—Donold St. Germain, Jenerette, 17-12
Sailfish—Jeanne Moreau Barillas, San Salvadore, 66-0
Shark—Edward Lorraine, Golden Meadow, 8 ft.-8½ in.
Sheepshead—Terry Serrigney, Leesville, 6-14
Spadefish—Rosemary Heinz, Metairie, 5-9
Speckled Trout—Francis Federine, Golden Meadow, 6-8½
Triple Tail—Colty Callis, Buras, 21-0
Yellow Fin Tuna—Jim Trotter, New Orleans, 150-8
   (New record, old record held by Richard Brown of New Orleans-146-8 set in 1966)
Wahoo—Dr. R. Rein, *South Pass, 47-14

SCUBA DIVISION

Grouper—Lolyd I. Scanllan, New Orleans, 16-8
Amberjack—Alvin Dufrene, Des Allemonds, 48-12
Cobia—Jerry Bourgeouis, Westwego, 38-4
Jack Crevalle—Alvin Dufrene, Des Allemonds, 25-12
Barracuda—A. L. Manet, Jr., Westwego, 25-12
Red Snapper—Al Juul, New Orleans, 18-8
Sheepshead—Malcom Theriot, New Orleans, 5-9

*These fish were weighed in at the South Pass Weighing Station and some home town names were unavailable.

Louisiana's 1967-68 Hunting Seasons
and
Wildlife Management Area Regulations

1967-68 HUNTING SEASONS
The Louisiana Wild Life and Fisheries Commission today released in full the 1967-68 deer hunting regulations and regulations for deer, small game, game birds and wild turkeys on its game management areas.

RESIDENT GAME BIRDS AND ANIMALS

(Shooting Hours—one-half hour before sunrise to one-half hour after sunset)
Quail: November 23—February 28; Daily Bag 10; Possession 20.

Rabbit: October 7—February 11; Daily Bag 8; Possession 16.

Squirrel: October 7—January 10; Daily Bag 8; Possession 16.

Bear: Closed.

Turkey: March 30—April 21; Daily Bag 1, Gobblers only; Season Limit 2.

Deer: See Deer Hunting Schedule.

Archery Season: October 7—January 10, 1966, Inclusive (See Deer Hunting Schedule). Season Limit 3.

Commercial Hunting Preserves: October 1—March 31, Pen-raised birds only.

1967-68 MIGRATORY REGULATIONS

Doves: 3 way split; September 2-September 17, 16 days; October 14-November 23, 41 days; December 19-December 31, 13 days; Bag Limit 12; Possession 24.

Teal: Experimental Season, September 22-September 30. Daily Bag limit 4, possession 8, Blue-Winged and Green-Winged Teal only. Each hunter must have in possession while hunting:

1. Special teal hunting permit (application deadline August 23).
2. Basic hunting license or State hunting permit except persons under 16 years of age.
3. Federal duck stamp except persons under 16 years of age.

Rails: November 4-January 12, 1968; Bag limit on King and Clapper and larger rails 15; possession 30. On Sora and Virginia rails Bag Limit 15; Possession 30. Aggregate of 30 or Possession of 60.

Woodcock: November 25-January 28, 1968, Bag limit 5; Possession of 10.

Snipe (Wilson's): November 25-January 13; Bag limit 8; Possession 16.

SHOOTING HOURS:

1. Doves: 1:00 P.M. to sunset through October 28 and 12 noon to sunset for remainder of season.
2. Rails, Gallinules, Snipe and Woodcock; one-half hour before sunrise to sunset.

1967-68 DEER HUNTING SCHEDULE

A. Bag: One legal deer per day; three legal deer per season.
B. Legal buck is defined as a deer with antlers not less than three inches in length. The killing of bucks with antlers less than three inches and doe deer is prohibited except where specifically permitted.

C. Deer hunting restricted to legal bucks, only, except where otherwise specifically permitted.

D. Either sex deer, or any deer, is defined as any male or female deer, except spotted fawns which are protected, taken in any area designated and regulated as such.

E. Still Hunting only prohibits the use of dogs for hunting or the training of dogs in areas so designated, including game management or refuge areas. In all other areas, deer hunting will be permitted with or without the use of dogs.

F. All areas not specifically designated as being open are hereby closed.

G. Archery Season: October 7-January 10, 1968, inclusive. Either sex deer may be taken in all areas declared open for deer hunting, including game management areas. During periods that any area is open for gun hunting for deer, archery hunters are restricted to the same regulations that apply to gun hunters, and this also applies to wildlife management areas. No archery season on the Red Dirt Game Management Area. Archery season restricted on the Thistlewaite and Zemurray Park Game Management Areas. For details, see provisions under game management area schedule. Special bow and arrow regulations: Arrows used for hunting deer shall have well sharpened metal broadhead blades not less than 7/8 inch in width.

The following shall be unlawful:

1. To have in possession any gun while hunting with bow and arrow during the special bow and arrow deer season.
2. To have in possession or under control while hunting, any poisoned arrows, arrows with explosive tips, or any bow drawn, held or released by mechanical means.
3. To hunt deer with a bow having a pull less than 30 pounds.

H. All deer or parts thereof shall be tagged as provided by law.

DESCRIPTION OF AREAS

40 Days with or Without Dogs:
    November 24-December 17
    December 26-January 10, 1968

AREA NO. 1: All or parts of Richland, Madison*, Franklin, Tensas, Concordia, St. Landry, Pointe Coupee, West Feliciana, West Baton Rouge, Lafayette, St. Martin, Iberville, Vermilion, Iberia, Assumption, Ascension, St. Mary, St. James, St. John, Terrebonne, Lafourche, St. Charles, Jetterson, Plaquemines, St. Bernard, Orleans, St. Tammany, Tangipahoa, Livingston, and Avoyelles Parishes.

East of Cameron-Vermilion parish line from Gulf of Mexico to La. Hwy. 14, south of La. Hwy. 14 to New Iberia, east of U.S. Hwy. 90 from New Iberia to Lafayette, east of U.S. Hwy. 167 from Lafayette to Opelousas, south of U.S. Hwy. 190 from Opelousas to junction of U.S. Hwy. 71, east of U.S. Hwy. 71 from U.S. Hwy. 190 to Bunkie, south and east of La. Hwy. 115 from Bunkie to Marksville to Red River, south and east of Red River from La. Hwy. 115 to Black River, south and east of Black River from Red River to its junction with U.S. Hwy. 84 at Jonesville, east of Black, Ouachita and Boeuf Rivers to Deer Creek, east of Deer Creek to La. Hwy. 15, east of La. Hwy. 15 to Winnsboro, east of La. Hwy. 17 from Winnsboro to U.S. Hwy. 80, south of U.S. Hwy. 80 from La. Hwy. 17 to the Mississippi River. West of the Mississippi River from the Arkansas line to La. Hwy. 22 in Ascension parish, south of La. Hwy. 22 from the Mississippi River to Sorrento to Springfield to the Tchefuncte River, west of Tchefuncte River from La. Hwy. 22 to Lake Pontchartrain, west of Lake Pontchartrain from Tchefuncte River to Pass Manchac, north of Pass Manchac to U.S. Hwy. 51, west of U.S. Hwy. 51 to La. Hwy. 638 (Frenier Beach Road) south of La. Hwy. 638 from U.S. Hwy. 51 to Lake Pontchartrain, south of Lake Pontchartrain and Lake Borgne to the Mississippi Sound.*

*The taking of either sex deer will be legal during the first five days of the first segment and also during the first five days of the second segment of the regular deer season in that portion of Madison parish south of U.S. Hwy. 80, and in all of Tensas Parish except Ward 3. Diamond Point and Sargents Point are included in the open area.

. **33 Days With or Without Dogs:**
    November 24-December 10
    December 26-January 10, 1968

AREA NO. 2: All or parts of Madison, East Carroll*, West Carroll, Morehouse, Richland and Ouachita.
North of U.S. Hwy. 80 from Mississippi State Line to Hwy. 17 at Delhi, east of La. Hwy. 17 to Pioneer, north of La. Hwy. 588 from Pioneer to Boeuf River, west of Boeuf River to La. Hwy. 134, north of La. Hwy. 134 to La. Hwy. 133 at Oak Ridge, west of La. Hwy. 133 from Oak Ridge to U.S. Hwy. 80, north of U.S. Hwy. 80 from La. Hwy. 133 to Bayou Lafourche, east of Bayou Lafourche to Little Bayou Boeuf, east and north of Little Bayou Boeuf to La. Hwy. 2 at Perryville, north and west of La. Hwy. 2 from Perryville to the Ouachita River at Sterlington, east of Ouachita Diver to Arkansas Line.*

*The taking of either sex deer will be legal during the first five days of first segment of the regular season in that portion of East Carroll Parish lying east of the main line Mississippi River levee.

AREA NO. 3: All or parts of Beauregard and Calcasieu Parishes.
South of Anacoco Bayou from the Texas line to La. Hwy. 111, west of La. Hwy. 111 to U.S. Hwy. 190, south of U.S. Hwy. 190 from La. Hwy. 111 to DeRidder; west of La. Hwy. 27

La. Hwy. 9 to La. Hwy. 155, south of La. Hwy. 155 to Saline, west of La. Hwy. 9 to Junction of La. Hwy. 126 to · Dugdemona Bayou, east of Dugdemona Bayou to La. Hwy. 4. south of La. Hwy. 4 from Dugdemona Bayou to Jonesboro to Chatham to Vixen, west of Parish Road from Vixen to La. Hwy. 126, north of La. Hwy. 126 to La. Hwy. 127, west of La. Hwy. 127 to U.S. Hwy. 165, west of U.S. Hwy. 165 to Little River, west of Little River and Saline Bayou to La. Hwy. 28, south of La. Hwy. 28 from Saline Bayou to junction of U.S. Hwy. 84, south and east of U.S. Hwy. 84 to Black River. west of Black River to Red River. north of Red River from Black River to La. Hwy. 8 at Boyce, north of La. Hwy. 8 from Boyce to Flatwoods, north of La. Hwy. 119 from Flatwoods to Goram, north of La. Hwy. 118 from Goram to Kisatchie, west of La. Hwy. 117 from Kisatchie to Leesville, north of La. Hwy. 8 from Leesville to Texas line (Sabine River), east of Texas line to Logansport.*

*All private lands surrounded by the Saline Wildlife Management Area are subject to the same regulations established for the Saline Wildlife Management Area proper except no permit is required to hunt these enclosed private lands.

AREA NO. 5: All or parts of Rapides, Beauregard, Allen, Evangeline, St. Landry, Vernon and Avoyelles Parishes.

South and east of La. Hwys. 28, 112, 113 and 112 from Alexandria to Union Hill to Sugartown to U.S. Hwy. 171; east of U.S. Hwy. 171 from La. Hwy. 112 to Ragley, north of U.S. Hwy. 190 from Ragley to Opelousas, west of U.S. 167 from Opelousas to Ville Platte, west of La. Hwy. 29 from Ville Platte to Bunkie, west of U.S. Hwy. 71 from Bunkie to Alexandria.

23 Days With or Without Dogs:
November 24-December 3
December 26-January 7, 1968

AREA NO. 6: Parts of East Feliciana, West Feliciana and East Baton Rouge Parishes.

West of La. Hwy. 969 from the Mississippi line to the junction of La. Hwy. 66, west of La. Hwy. 66 from the junction of La. Hwy. 969 to the junction of U.S. Hwy. 61, west of U.S. Hwy. 61 from the junction of La. Hwy. 66 to La. Hwy. 64, north of La. Hwy. 64 from U.S. Hwy. 61 to the Mississippi River at Port Hickey, east of the Mississippi River from Port Hickey to the Mississippi Line.

AREA NO. 7: Parts of St. Helena,

East of La. Hwy. 450 from the Mississippi State line to La. Hwy. 10, south of La. Hwy. 10 from La. Hwy. 450 to Tchefuncte River, east of the Tchefuncte River from La. Hwy. 10 to Lake Ponchartrain, north of Lake Ponchartrain and Lake Borgne from Tchefuncte River to the Mississippi line.

east of La. Hwy. 25 from Franklinton to the Mississippi line.

AREA NO. 9: All or parts of Winn, Morehouse, Jackson, Caldwell, Ouachita, Franklin, Catahoula, LaSalle, Union, Lincoln and Richland Parishes. West of Ouachita River from Arkansas line to Sterlington, south of La. Hwy. 2 from Sterlington to Perryville, south and west of Little Boeuf Bayou from Perryville to Lafourche Drainage Canal, west of Lafourche Drainage Canal to U.S. Hwy. 80, south of U.S. Hwy. 80 to La. Hwy. 133, east of La. Hwy. 133 to La. Hwy. 134, South of La. Hwy. 134 to La. Hwy. 183, west of La. Hwy. 183 to U.S. Hwy. 80, north of U.S. Hwy. 80 from Holly Ridge to Rayville, west of La. Hwy. 137 from Rayville to Archibald, west of La. Hwy. 15 from Archibald to Deer Creek, west of Deer Creek and Ouachita River to Jonesville, north of U.S. Hwy. 84 from Jonesville to La. Hwy. 28, north of La. Hwy. 28 to Saline Bayou, east of Saline Bayou and Little River to junction of U.S. Hwy. 165, east of U.S. Hwy. 165 from Little River to junction of La. Hwy. 127, north of La. Hwy. 127 to junction of La. Hwy. 126, south of La. Hwy. 126 to Parish Road from Chester to Vixen, north of La. Hwy. 4 from Vixen to Jonesboro, east of U.S. Hwy. 167 from Jonesboro to Arkansas line.

32 Days

10 Days With or Without Dogs:
November 24-December 3, 1967
9 Days Still Hunt Only
December 16-24, 1967
13 Days With or Without Dogs
December 26-January 7, 1968

AREA NO. 10: All or parts of Caddo, Webster, Claiborne, DeSoto, Red River, Union, Bienville, Jackson, Winn, Lincoln, Sabine, Natchitoches and Bossier Parishes.

West of U.S. Hwy. 167 from Arkansas line to Jonesboro, north of La. Hwy. 4 from Jonesboro to Dugdemona Creek to La. Hwy. 126, north of La. Hwy. 126 to La. Hwy. 9, east of La. Hwy. 9 from La. Hwy. 126 to La. Hwy. 155, north of La. Hwy. 155 to Mill to Readhimer to Saline to Ashland to Black Bayou, west of Black Lake to La. Hwy. 9, north of La. Hwy. 9 from Black Lake to intersection of U.S. Hwy. 71 and U.S.

AREA NO. 11: Portions of St. John Parish.

That portion of St. John Parish south of Pass Manchac from Lake Pontchartrain to U.S. Hwy. 51, east of U.S. Hwy. 51 from Pass Manchac to La. Hwy. 638 (Frenier Beach Road) north of La. Hwy. 638 from U.S. Hwy. 51 to Lake Pontchartrain, west of the shore of Lake Pontchartrain from La. Hwy. 638 to Pass Manchac.

14 Days Still Hunting Only:
November 24-28
December 16-24, 1967

AREA NO. 12: Parts of Natchitoches, Vernon, Beauregard, Calcasieu, Jefferson Davis, Allen, Rapides and Avoyelles Parishes.

East of La. Hwy. 117 from Leesville to Kisatchie, south of La. Hwy. 118 (Kisatchie-Mink-Gorum Road) from Kisatchie to Gorum, south of La. Hwy. 119 from Gorum to Flatwoods, south and east of La. Hwy. 8 from Flatwoods to Boyce, south and west of Red River from Boyce to La. Hwy. 115, west of La. Hwy. 115 from Red River to Bunkie, east of U.S. Hwy. 71 from Bunkie to Alexandria, north and west of La. Hwy. 28 from Alexandria to junction of La. Hwy. 112, west of La. Hwy. 112 from the junction of La. Hwy. 28 to Union Hill, north of La. Hwy. 113 from Union Hill to Sugartown, north of La. Hwy. 112 from Sugartown to the junction of U.S. Hwy. 171, west of U.S. Hwy. 171 from the junction of La. Hwy. 112 to Ragley south of U.S. Hwy. 190 from Ragley to Kinder west of U.S. Hwy. 165 from Kinder to Iowa, south of U.S. Hwy. 90 from Iowa to Welch, west of La. Hwy. 99 from Welch to La. Hwy. 14 north and east of La. Hwy. 14 from the junction of La. Hwy. 99 through Hayes and Holmwood to U.S. Hwy. 90, north of U.S. Hwy. 90 from the junction of La. Hwy. 14 to Sulphur east of La. Hwy. 27 from· Sulphur to DeRidder, north of U.S. Hwy. 190 from DeRidder to La. Hwy. 111, east of La. Hwy. 111 to Anacoco Bayou north of Anacoco Bayou from La. Hwy. 111 to the Texas line, east of Texas line from Anacoco Bayou to La. Hwy. 8, south of La. Hwy. 8 from the Texas line to Leesville.

10 Days Still Hunting Only:
November 24-December 3, 1967

AREA NO. 13: Parts of West Carroll, Richland and Franklin Parishes. West of La. Hwy. 17 from Pioneer to junction of La. Hwy. 132 in Franklin Parish, north and west of La. Hwy. 132 from junction of La.

Hwy. 17 to La. Hwy. 137, east of La. Hwy. 137 from its junction with La. Hwy. 132 to Rayville, south. of U.S. Hwy. 80 from Rayville to Holly Ridge, east of La. Hwy. 183 from Holly Ridge to junction of La. Hwy. 134, north and east of La. Hwy. 134 from junction of La. Hwy. 183 to Boeuf River, east of Boeuf River from La. Hwy. 134 to La. Hwy. 588, south of La. Hwy. 588 from Boeuf River to Pioneer.

5 Days Still Hunting Only:
November 24-November 28, 1967

AREA NO. 14: Part of Cameron Parish.

South and east of Mermentau River from the Gulf of Mexico to Grand Lake, south of Grand Lake, Callicon Lake and Old Intracoastal Canal to the Cameron-Vermilion Parish Line, west of Cameron-Vermilion Parish line from the Old Intracoastal Canal to the Gulf of Mexico.

10 Days With or Without Dogs:
November 24-November 28
December 26-December 30, 1967

AREA NO. 15: Parts of Ascension, East Baton Rouge and Livingston Parishes.

West of La. Hwy. 447 from Walker to Port Vincent, north of La. Hwy. 42 from Port Vincent to U.S. Hwy. 61, east of U.S. Hwy. 61 from junction of La. Hwy. 42 to Bayou Manchac, north of Bayou Manchac from U.S. Hwy. 61 to the Mississippi River, east of the Mississippi River from Bayou Manchac to U.S. Hwy. 190, south of U.S. Hwy. 190 from the Mississippi River to Walker.

GAME MANAGEMENT AREAS SCHEDULE
1967-68

For all Game Management Areas, except as otherwise specified:

DEER: 5 days of deer hunting unless otherwise specified: November 24-November 26, 1967; either sex until the designated number of deer are taken, after which the remaining days of the first 3 days, if any, shall be open to "bucks only" hunting. Notification of type of hunt to be held will be made when daily permit is obtained. Two (2) additional days of "bucks only" hunting will be allowed on December 2 and December 3, 1967.

PERMITS: When daily permits are required these may be obtained at the permit stations located on or near the Game Management Areas.

Season permits, where required, may be obtained in advance beginning August 25 from any Commission District Office; P. O. Box 915, Minden; P. O. Box 4004, Ouachita Station, Monroe; P. O. Box 278, Tioga; P. O. Box 426, Ferriday; P. O. Box 405, DeRidder; P. O. Box 585, Opelousas; P. O. Box 14526, Southeast Station, Baton Rouge; 400 Royal Street, New Orleans.

Turkey Season permits obtained at District Offices listed above beginning March 1, 1968.

The use of dogs is prohibited except for bird hunting. All deer killed on Game Management Areas where daily permits are issued must be validated at a deer weighing station. Archery season closed on November 23 and December 1, 1967, on all Game Management Areas.

ALEXANDER STATE FOREST:
Deer: 50 any deer and 3 days, No-

Louisiana Wildlife Management Areas

vember 24-26, Daily Permit. Bucks only, December 2-3, 1967, Daily permit.
Squirrel & Rabbits: October 7-November 5, Season Permit, Check locally for restricted areas.

BODCAU:
Deer: Same as outside EXCEPT still hunt only, Season permit.
All Small Game: Same as outside but still hunt only, including waterfowl, season permit.
Dogs allowed only for bird hunting.
No permanent duck blinds.
No quail hunting on marked Foreign Game Bird Experimental Area.

CALDWELL:
Deer: 3 days, November 24-26, Bucks only, Daily Permit, Bucks only, December 2-3, Daily permits.
Squirrel & Rabbits: October 7-November 5, Season permit.
Waterfowl: Same as outside season, EXCEPT no waterfowl hunting during deer season and no permanent duck blinds, Season permit.

CATAHOULA:
Deer: 200 any deer and 3 days, November 24-26, Daily permits. Bucks only December 2-3, Daily permits.
Squirrels & Rabbits: October 7-November 5, Season permits.
Quail: January 6-February 28, 1968, Season permits.
Woodcock: January 6-January 28, 1968, Season permit.

CANEY (MIDDLE FORK & CORNEY):
Deer: Same as outside EXCEPT still hunt only, Season Permit.
All Small Game: Same as outside but still hunt only, Season Permit.
Dogs allowed only for bird hunting.
No permanent duck blinds.

CITIES SERVICE:
Deer: Same as outside season, EXCEPT still hunt only, Season Permit.
Quail: January 6-February 28, 1968. Season Permit.
Woodcock: January 6-January 28, 1968, Season Permit.
Squirrel & Rabbit: Same as outside season, still hunt only, season permit.

CONCORDIA:
Deer: Bucks only 3 days, November 24-26, Daily Permit, December 2-3. Bucks only, Daily Permit.
Squirrel & Rabbit: October 7-November 19, Season permit.
Waterfowl: Same as outside season, EXCEPT no waterfowl hunting during deer season and no permanent duck blinds, season permit.

EVANGELINE:
Deer: 50 any deer and 3 days, November 24-26, Daily permit. Bucks only 2 days, December 2-3, Daily permit.
Squirrel & Rabbit: October 7-November 5, Season permit.
Quail: January 6-February 28, 1968, Season permit.
Woodcock: January 6-February 28, 1968, Season permit.

FORT POLK:*
Deer: 400 any deer and 3 days, November 24-26, Daily permit. Legal bucks only, concurrent with adjacent areas, Season permit.
All Small Game: Same as outside season. Bird dogs permitted only to hunt birds EXCEPT no dogs allowed on November 24, 25, 26.

*Military Clearance required in addition to season permit—check locally.

GEORGIA-PACIFIC:
Deer: 3 days, November 24-26, first day any deer, remainder bucks only, Daily permits. December 2-3 Bucks only, Daily permits.
Squirrel & Rabbit: October 7-October 29, still hunt only, Season permits.
Woodcock and Quail: December 23-31, 1967, Season permits.
Turkey: March 30-April 7, 1968, Daily Permit.

JACKSON-BIENVILLE:
Deer: 250 any deer and 3 days, November 24-26, Daily permit. Bucks only 2 days, December 2-3, Daily permit.
Squirrel & Rabbit: October 7-31, Season permit.
Quail: January 6-February 28, 1968, Season permit.
Woodcock: January 6-January 28, 1968, Season permit.

Deer: 225 any deer and 3 days, November 24-26, Daily permit. Bucks only, December 2-3, Daily permit.
Squirrel & Rabbit: October 7-November 5, Season permit.
Quail: January 6-February 28, 1968, Season permit.
Woodcock: January 6-January 28, 1968, Season permit.

*No archery season due to deer trapping and research.

RED RIVER:
Deer: Same as outside, still hunting only, season permit.
Squirrel & Rabbit: Same as outside, still hunting only, Season permit.
Waterfowl: Same as outside, no permanent duck blinds, season permit.

RUSSELL SAGE:
Deer: 150 any deer and 3 days, November 24-26, Daily permit.
Bucks only, 2 days, December 2-3, Daily permit. Remainder concurrent with outside area EXCEPT still hunting only, Season permit.
All Small Game: Same as outside but still hunt only.

SABINE:
Deer: 50 any deer and 3 days, November 24-26, Daily Permit. Bucks only, December 2-3, Daily permit.
Squirrel & Rabbit: October 7-November 5, Season permit.
Woodcock: January 6-January 28, 1968, Season permit.
Quail: January 6-February 28, 1968, Season permit.

SALINE:
Deer: Bucks only 3 days, November 24-26, Daily Permit, Bucks only December 2-3, Daily permit.
Squirrel and Rabbit: October 7-November 19, Season Permit.
Waterfowl: Same as outside season, EXCEPT no waterfowl hunting during deer season and no permanent duck blinds, Season permit.
All hunting closed within marked study areas.

SODA LAKE:
Waterfowl hunting permitted Monday, Wednesday and Saturday mornings only (until 12 noon) throughout waterfowl season, to include experimental teal season, Season permit.
Small game seasons open during statewide season EXCEPT no hunting allowed during the closed portions of waterfowl seasons. No permanent duck blinds.

SPRING BAYOU:
Deer: Bucks only, 3 days, November 24-26, Daily permit. Bucks only, 2 days, December 2-3, Daily permit.

Deer: 80 any deer and 3 days, November 24-26, Daily permit. Bucks only, 2 days, December 2-3, Daily permit.
Squirrel & Rabbit: October 7-November 5, Season permit.
Woodcock: January 6-January 28, 1968, Season permit.
Quail: January 6-February 28, 1968, Season permit.

WEST BAY:
Deer: 3 days, November 24-26, First day any deer, Daily permit. Bucks only December 2-3, Daily permit.
Squirrel & Rabbit: October 7-November 5, Season permit.
Woodcock: December 26-January 28, 1968, Season permit.
Quail: December 26-February 28, 1968, Season permit.
Turkey: March 30-31, 1968, Gobblers only, Daily permit.

ZEMURRAY PARK:
Deer: December 11, 12, and 13, Any deer, 200 hunters per day. Non-transferable permits are to be issued by mail in advance of hunts. Louisiana resident hunters only to be selected at public drawing in Baton

will void all his applications. No small game hunting permitted.
Archery: Hunting of Deer with bow and arrow permitted each Saturday and Sunday (weekends) beginning October 1, ending November 26, 1967, Daily permit.

PASS-A-LOUTRE: (Waterfowl Management Area)
Waterfowl hunting only, fee $5.00 for two-day hunt, mail application along with check or money order to Refuge Division, Louisiana Wild Life and Fisheries Commission, 400 Royal Street, New Orleans, Louisiana 70130 for drawing according to schedule to be announced. Accommodations for men only 16 years or older. Seasons permit available for adjacent open portion of area free of charge.

TRAPPING SEASON

The trapping season on all Louisiana furbearers is as follows: December 1, 1967 through February 28, 1968 and will apply to Nutria, Beaver, Mink, Muskrat, Otter, Raccoon, Opossum and Skunk.

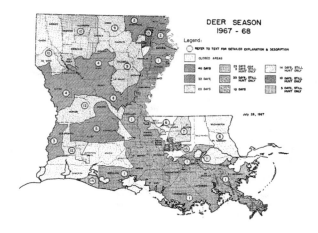

DEER SEASON
1967 - 68

Legend:
REFER TO TEXT FOR DETAILED EXPLANATION & DESCRIPTION
CLOSED AREAS
40 DAYS
33 DAYS
23 DAYS
23 DAYS ANY
3 DAYS, STILL
HUNT ONLY
33 DAYS, STILL
HUNT ONLY
10 DAYS
14 DAYS, STILL
HUNT ONLY
10 DAYS, STILL
HUNT ONLY
5 DAYS, STILL
HUNT ONLY

July 26, 1967

Commission Issues Strong Protest of Proposed
Coast Guard Boundary Line Changes in Gulf

THE LOUISIANA WILD LIFE AND FISHERIES Commission revealed highlights of its protest against proposed changes by the U. S. Coast Guard in the line of demarcation between inland and international waters.

The formal protest was filed in writing by the commission at public hearings held in Morgan City and in New Orleans on Friday, August 4, and Monday, August 7.

"The Coast Guard claims that the changes are needed to simplify navigational procedures for fishing vessels," the official protest read, "and to enhance enforcement against any infractions of such rules. In view of conditions along the Louisiana coast, we cannot understand how such a proposal can be justified.

"For example, Louisiana has some 6,283 local commercial shrimp boats operating in its waters. Of this number of boats, 3,958 or 63 per cent are under thirty feet in length and probably never work out to the present line of demarcation between inland and international waters.

"The remaining 2,375, making up 37 per cent of the shrimp fleet, is theoretically capable of operating beyond the present boundary line of inland waters, but it is reliably estimated that not more than 300 to 500 of these larger boats actually fish in the vicinity of the boundary line, or beyond it to any extent."

This being the case, it was pointed out, more than 90 per cent of all of the present shrimping operations falls within the inland waters of the state, while only 10 per cent or less of their operators must be equipped and/or educated to operate beyond the boundary in international waters.

By arbitrarily moving the boundary line to the very beaches and shore lines of this state it will necessitate that practically 100 per cent of the fishing fleet will have to be equipped for frequent passage from inland waters to international waters and that the crews and pilots will have to become aware of the necessary procedures for frequent passage from one area to another, the commission's protest continued.

The protest also pointed out that in addition to 6,000 or more commercial fishing vessels operating in Louisiana waters, there are some 40,000 pleasure and recreational craft located in an area below U. S. Highway 190, all of which are from time to time operated within the inland waters of the state.

"While most of the smaller pleasure boats rarely sail far enough from shore to be involved in international waters as presently defined, the proposed rule change would mean that a myriad of pleasure and recreational craft and small commercial boats would be faced with the possibility of crossing from inland to international waters on a frequent basis," the protest read.

The commission further expounded upon its inability to understand how the proposed change to the coast line could do anything but cause hardship, as well as present an insurmountable problem as far as enforcement was concerned.

It was pointed out that the Louisiana Wild Life and Fisheries has a tremendous responsibility in regulating and controlling fisheries in the inshore and near shore waters and there is a definite possibility that control might be lost legally as far as enforcement or regulations are concerned.

"In one extreme facet of this proposal we find that over three thousand acres of privately leased oyster bottoms and an additional five thousand acres of applications for such leases which will be arbitrarily placed in international waters," the protest continued.

The possible loss of part of the authority to management of the 40 to 50 million dollar industry by the Louisiana Wild Life and Fisheries Commission presents a serious threat to this vast fisheries resource which includes shrimp, oysters, finfish and menhaden and there is no alternative but to add this protest to that of many other industries and organizations. ❋

Wildlife Shorts

New Jersey is installing 980 mirrors along stretches of the Garden State Parkway as part of an unusual experiment. The mirrors will reflect headlight beams into fields along the super highway. The experiment, based on the principle that deer are reluctant to cross light beams, has succeeded in parts of Europe and has saved lives of many motorists and animals.

Butterflies number about 700 species in North America, north of Mexico. Lepidoptera (butterflies) means "scaly winged" and refers to the fact that the hairs covering the wings are flattened or scaly-like and give color to the wing.

Among Cajuns of Louisiana, pompano is the unchallenged favorite. No group searches out pompano with greater dedication, cooks it with greater care, or eats it with greater relish.

Veteran Louisiana charter-boat skippers look upon the offshore oil rigs as bottomless cornucopias, continually attracting new fish to replace those removed by anglers.

Charles R. Shaw

THE SPRING AND FALL migrations of water-fowl have always held a great deal of interest for sportsmen and for many others as well. There is still the fascination of observing the physical manifestation of one of natures better guarded secrets, one which has never been fully and satisfactorily explained by man in spite of his vast array of scientific knowledge and technical achievements.

The Blue-winged Teal is one of the earliest ducks to move south, arriving in Louisiana as early as August but staying only a short while before going on to Central and South America. In fact, by the time that the majority of other waterfowl have arrived in Louisiana, most of the Blue-winged Teal have moved on to the warmer climates for the winter.

Although a few of these small ducks nest in Louisiana, being one of the few species known to breed in our state, and some spend the winter with us, by far the majority must be considered as transients, passing through on their fall and spring flights.

The name of this bird is descriptive, of course, referring to the large chalky blue wing patch on the forepart of the wings of both sexes. The green speculum at the rear of the wing is inconspicuous in flight, the large light blue wing patch in front of it, catching the eye of the observer. In adult males in full plumage, the crescent-shaped white markings on the side of the slaty gray head easily identify the bird. It is a bit more difficult to spot the females and immatures which are a mottled brown with sort of whitish underparts. Also at the time of their passage through Louisiana most of the males are in eclipse plumage and resemble the females anyway. Blue-wings are one of the latest species to change into full breeding plumage, usually not completing the change until late winter. These birds belong to the group known as "dabbling ducks", which includes such well known species as the mallard, pintail, gadwall, etc., and which feed primarily in shallow water areas where their type of feeding contrasts markedly with the deep diving habits of such birds as the Canvas-backs, Red-heads and Scaup. The latter, of course, being able to utilize the deeper lakes and estuaries. The Bluewing deviates a bit from the well known "tip-up" technique used by most of the dabbling ducks and could be classified as surface feeders, merely taking what food they can reach by stretching out the neck to the fullest extent.

BLUE-WINGED TEAL

Anas discors

The nest is well made of soft grasses lined with down and by utilizing a hollow for the nesting site the top of the nest is kept down near ground level, rendering it less conspicuous. Nests are located not too far from water and are generally well concealed. The usual clutch will consist of 8-10 creamy white eggs, although considerable variation can occur both in clutch size and in the coloration of the eggs.

The downy young hatch in about 22 days and are usually taken to the water shortly after hatching, certainly on the same day. Since these are late nesting birds with an early fall migration departure date, growth is necessarily rapid and the young birds can fly at about six weeks.

The closely related Cinnamon Teal has been recorded from Louisiana and due to the similarity of the females and immatures it is probable that a much larger number occur than have been reported. Of course, the male is easily spotted if in full plumage since he is colored a very noticeable cinnamon-red.

Since conservation always includes the wise use connation, Louisiana has been in the forefront of the fight to have an early season so that these waterfowl may be utilized more fully by the sportsmen. This has culminated in the special teal season which is now in its third year. This year it runs from September 22nd through the 30th and a special free permit must be used in addition to license and stamp. If the sportsmen of the state abide by all the rules and regulations, it is quite probable that this season will become a permanent fixture. ✱

Illustration by Sidney A. Gautreaux, Jr.

Photo by Robert Dennie

RABBIT HUNTING PROVIDES TOP SPORT IN LOUISIANA AND STATE HUNTERS HAVE A LENGTHY SEASON

Beagles At Work

Possibly the greatest number of hunters begin their hunting careers by hunting rabbits. It would be a toss up between rabbits and squirrels. Those early experiences are never forgotten and in later years rabbit hunting continues to be a popular sport, not only at a national level but throughout Louisiana. State rabbit hunters have the opportunity to hunt the smaller cottontails such as are shown here, or their larger cousins, the swamp rabbits. It's a gratifying sport and rabbits have great appeal when prepared for the table.

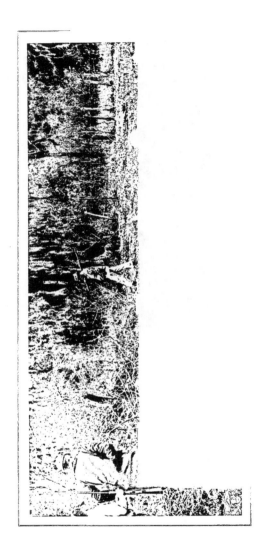